A Gift from the
Lammie Williams Fund

RYE FREE READING ROOM
Escape to the Library

COMPUTER MATH

MATH 24/7

Banking Math

Business Math

Computer Math

Culinary Math

Fashion Math

Game Math

Shopping Math

Sports Math

Time Math

Travel Math

MATH 24/7

COMPUTER MATH

JAMES FISCHER

Mason Crest

Mason Crest
450 Parkway Drive, Suite D
Broomall, PA 19008
www.masoncrest.com

Printed in the United States of America.

First printing
9 8 7 6 5 4 3 2 1

Series ISBN: 978-1-4222-2901-9
ISBN: 978-1-4222-2904-0
ebook ISBN: 978-1-4222-8915-0

The Library of Congress has cataloged the
    hardcopy format(s) as follows:

        Library of Congress Cataloging-in-Publication Data

Fischer, James, 1988-
  Computer math / James Fischer.
      pages cm. – (Math 24/7)
  Includes bibliographical references and index.
    ISBN 978-1-4222-2904-0 (hardcover) – ISBN 978-1-4222-2901-9 (series) – ISBN 978-1-4222-8915-0 (ebook)
  1. Computer science–Mathematics–Juvenile literature. 2. Computer programming–Juvenile literature. 3. Web sites–Design–Juvenile literature. 4. Computers–Juvenile literature. I. Title.
  QA76.9.M35F57 2014
  004.01'51–dc23
                    2013015660

Produced by Vestal Creative Services.
www.vestalcreative.com

Contents

INTRODUCTION

How would you define math? It's not as easy as you might think. We know math has to do with numbers. We often think of it as a part, if not the basis, for the sciences, especially natural science, engineering, and medicine. When we think of math, most of us imagine equations and blackboards, formulas and textbooks.

But math is actually far bigger than that. Think about examples like Polykleitos, the fifth-century Greek sculptor, who used math to sculpt the "perfect" male nude. Or remember Leonardo da Vinci? He used geometry—what he called "golden rectangles," rectangles whose dimensions were visually pleasing—to create his famous *Mona Lisa*.

Math and art? Yes, exactly! Mathematics is essential to disciplines as diverse as medicine and the fine arts. Counting, calculation, measurement, and the study of shapes and the motions of physical objects: all these are woven into music and games, science and architecture. In fact, math developed out of everyday necessity, as a way to talk about the world around us. Math gives us a way to perceive the real world—and then allows us to manipulate the world in practical ways.

For example, as soon as two people come together to build something, they need a language to talk about the materials they'll be working with and the object that they would like to build. Imagine trying to build something—anything—without a ruler, without any way of telling someone else a measurement, or even without being able to communicate what the thing will look like when it's done!

The truth is: We use math every day, even when we don't realize that we are. We use it when we go shopping, when we play sports, when we look at the clock, when we travel, when we run a business, and even when we cook. Whether we realize it or not, we use it in countless other ordinary activities as well. Math is pretty much a 24/7 activity!

And yet lots of us think we hate math. We imagine math as the practice of dusty, old college professors writing out calculations endlessly. We have this idea in our heads that math has nothing to do with real life, and we tell ourselves that it's something we don't need to worry about outside of math class, out there in the real world.

But here's the reality: Math helps us do better in many areas of life. Adults who don't understand basic math applications run into lots of problems. The Federal Reserve, for example, found that people who went bankrupt had an average of one and a half times more debt than their income—in other words, if they were making $24,000 per year, they had an average debt of $36,000. There's a basic subtraction problem there that should have told them they were in trouble long before they had to file for bankruptcy!

As an adult, your career—whatever it is—will depend in part on your ability to calculate mathematically. Without math skills, you won't be able to become a scientist or a nurse, an engineer or a computer specialist. You won't be able to get a business degree—or work as a waitress, a construction worker, or at a checkout counter.

Every kind of sport requires math too. From scoring to strategy, you need to understand math—so whether you want to watch a football game on television or become a first-class athlete yourself, math skills will improve your experience.

And then there's the world of computers. All businesses today—from farmers to factories, from restaurants to hair salons—have at least one computer. Gigabytes, data, spreadsheets, and programming all require math comprehension. Sure, there are a lot of automated math functions you can use on your computer, but you need to be able to understand how to use them, and you need to be able to understand the results.

This kind of math is a skill we realize we need only when we are in a situation where we are required to do a quick calculation. Then we sometimes end up scratching our heads, not quite sure how to apply the math we learned in school to the real-life scenario. The books in this series will give you practice applying math to real-life situations, so that you can be ahead of the game. They'll get you started—but to learn more, you'll have to pay attention in math class and do your homework. There's no way around that.

But for the rest of your life—pretty much 24/7—you'll be glad you did!

1
DOWNLOAD SPEEDS

Teresa just moved to a new city and a new house. She has picked out her new room, and her parents are decorating the rest of the house.

When they first moved in, they didn't have any computers set up. Then when Teresa's brother AJ unpacked his laptop, and her dad set up the family's computer, they discovered they didn't have Internet access. With all the things they had to do for the move, Teresa's parents had forgotten to get Internet service for their new home.

Teresa and her dad go to the local library where there are plenty of computers and free Internet. They look up what the best Internet deals are, so they can call and order an Internet package.

Teresa sees a lot of numbers she doesn't immediately understand. What does 512/128 Kb/s mean, for example? Her dad explains that those are the download and upload speeds. The first number shows how fast you can transfer information from another computer system onto your own. You can download music, spreadsheets, e-mail attachments, and a lot more.

You'll first need to understand how people write download speeds. Unfortunately, there isn't really a standard notation. People commonly use Kb/s for kilobits per second or Kbit/s. Megabits per second could be Mb/s or Mbit/s. They all mean the same thing.

If you are trying to download a file that is 67 megabits, you would be able to download it much faster with a higher speed, like 6 Mb/s. The download will be slower if your Internet download speed is 512 Kb/s.

Here are the steps you need to take to figure out just how long a file will take to download.

- Convert your download speed from kilobits or megabits per second to kilobytes or megabytes per second by dividing by 8. (This step will be explained more in section 3.)
- Make sure the file size is in the same units as the download speed. If it's not, use the information below to convert the numbers into the same unit of speed.

$$1024 \text{ bytes} = 1 \text{ kilobyte}$$
$$1024 \text{ kilobytes} = 1 \text{ megabyte}$$
$$1024 \text{ megabytes} = 1 \text{ gigabyte}$$

- Divide the file size by the download speed to get the number of seconds the download will take.

Now find how long a 980-kilobyte file would take to download at 6 Mb/s:
6 Mb/s ÷ 8 = .75 megabytes per second
980 kilobytes ÷ 1024 = .96 megabytes
.96 megabytes ÷ .75 megabytes per second= 1.28 seconds

1. How long would it take the file to download at 512 Kb/s?

2. Are either download speeds more than a second? Do you think you would notice the difference between the two speeds?

2
UPLOAD SPEEDS

Now that Teresa understands download speeds, she thinks she also gets upload speeds. Remember the second number in the Internet package offers? The second number in 512/128 Kb/s is the upload speed. Uploading means to transfer from your computer to another computer system. You can upload pictures to Facebook or videos onto YouTube.

Teresa and her dad need to figure out what upload speed they want. Once they decide, they can choose the right Internet package for them.

Upload speeds tend to be slower than download speeds. But, you can find how long it would take you to upload files at different upload speeds the same way you do with download speeds.

1. If you are trying to upload a file that is 12 megabytes, how long would it take in seconds to upload with the following upload speeds:

    560 Kb/s:

    2 Mb/s:

    1 Mb/s:

    128 Kb/s:

    5 Mb/s:

Now that Teresa can see that faster upload and download speeds mean she can add music to the computer faster and watch TV faster, she agrees with her dad that they shouldn't get the slowest Internet package. But how fast should they get?

Here are their choices:

    standard: 15/1 Mb/s, $40/month
    extra: 30/5 Mb/s, $50/month
    ultra: 50/5 Mb/s, $65/month

The very biggest files anyone will probably be downloading or uploading on the computer will be about 20 megabytes, which is fairly large, because Teresa's mom sometimes does some graphic design work.

2. How fast will 20 megabytes upload and download in each Internet package?

    standard:
    extra:
    ultra:

3. Teresa's parents don't really want to spend more than $50 a month. Which Internet package do you think they should get? Do you think they will notice the loss in speed if they don't order the ultra package?

3
COMPUTER STORAGE

Teresa and her dad go home, but it's too late to call the Internet company tonight—they're closed. Teresa sits down at the computer, but she doesn't really know what to do. She's used to surfing the Internet or watching her favorite TV shows online.

She clicks around, exploring all the buttons she's never used on the computer. At one point, she comes across a screen that shows her how much storage the computer has. She sees the words megabytes and gigabytes. They look awfully similar to the kilobits and megabits she learned about with download and upload speeds. She calls her brother AJ over, who explains that bytes, kilobytes, and megabytes are used to describe how much storage space a computer has. Unlike Internet speeds, which are given in bits, computer storage is expressed in bytes. Luckily, the two are related.

A bit is the smallest unit of information on a computer. A byte is just a little bigger—1 byte is actually 8 bits.

You can talk about bigger pieces of information on a computer, too. Kilobytes are bigger than bytes, megabytes are bigger than kilobytes, and so on. The chart below shows how all these units of measurement relate to each other:

8 bits = 1 byte
1024 bytes = 1 kilobyte
1024 kilobytes = 1 megabyte
1024 megabytes = 1 gigabyte
1024 gigabytes = 1 terabyte
1024 terabytes = 1 petabyte
1024 petabytes = 1 exabyte

1. How many kilobytes are in 1 gigabyte?

2. How many terabytes are in 3 exabytes?

The numbers can get pretty big!

When you are talking about a kilobit or megabit in Internet speed, you're really talking about a kilobyte or a megabyte divided by 8.

3. How many bits are in 89 bytes?

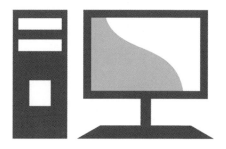

4
E-MAIL STORAGE

When Teresa's family sets up their Internet, the first thing Teresa does is check her e-mail. She's wondering if any of her friends from her old town have e-mailed her.

After she reads all her new e-mails, she notices a little bar in the corner of the screen that says 80% full. She has never really noticed it before, so she looks closer.

Sure enough, she also sees that it says "80% of your 10.1 GB full." More gigabytes! She already knows what that means in terms of how much space she has on her computer. Now she realizes her e-mail also has storage space for all her e-mails and e-mail attachments. On the next page, figure out how much storage space Teresa has used and how much she has left.

Teresa's e-mail program gives her 10.1 gigabytes of storage. To figure out how many gigabytes she has left, you'll have to work with percentages.

To find out how much 80% of 10.1 gigabytes is, convert the percentage into a decimal number by moving the decimal point two spaces to the left. Then 80% becomes .80. Multiply the decimal number by the total number of gigabytes, which tells you how much space Teresa has already used.

1. How much storage space has she used in gigabytes? How much space does she have left?

You can also turn the percentage into a fraction, to find out the answer another way. Put the percentage value over 100.

$$80\% = \frac{80}{100}$$

Then set the fraction equal to the number of gigabytes used in Teresa's e-mail, divided by the total number of gigabytes she started with. Use an X for the number of gigabytes she has used, because you don't know that number yet.

$$\frac{80}{10} = \frac{x}{100}$$

2. What do you get by cross-multiplying? Is it the same answer as before?

3. How many kilobytes has she used?

Teresa thinks she should delete some of her old e-mails to make more room for new e-mails. She goes through her really old e-mails and deletes 1924 megabytes worth of stuff.

4. How many gigabytes has her e-mail used up now? What percentage of space does she have now?

5

BINARY CODE

Teresa is wondering what bits and bytes and gigabytes actually are. She understands that they're ways to measure information in a computer, but what exactly are they measuring? How big is a bit to begin with? She asks AJ all these questions.

AJ tells her that she needs to understand binary code, the language that computers use. Computers can't easily understand the letters and numbers that humans use, so instead they store information as strings of 1s and 0s. Binary means "having only two states," and the binary code that computers use only has 1s or 0s.

The computer uses different combinations of these 1s and 0s to represent other characters. We'll talk more about that in chapter 6.

The word bit actually is short for binary digit. And one binary digit is the very smallest piece of computer language. A binary digit in computer language is a 0 or 1. You could say that 1 equals "on" or "yes," and 0 equals "off" or "no."

Counting looks different in binary than in our usual system for counting. We normally use a 10-digit system, made up of 10 digits (0 through 9). You can only count with two digits in binary code—but you need to count a lot higher than 2!

First, you need to be familiar with the idea of the powers of two. A power is a way of saying how many times you multiply a number by itself. Two to the power of 0 looks like 2^0 and equals 1. Two to the power of 1 looks like 2^1 and equals 2. Here are some more:

$$2^2 = 2 \times 2 = 4$$
$$2^3 = 2 \times 2 \times 2 = 8$$
$$2^4 = 2 \times 2 \times 2 \times 2 = 16$$

1. What is 2^7?

Here are the numbers 0 through 10 as they would be written in binary:

0000 (= 0)
0001 (= 1)
0010 (= 2)
0011 (= 3)
0100 (= 4)
0101 (= 5)

0110 (= 6)
0111 (= 7)
1000 (= 8)
1001 (= 9)
1010 (= 10)

To count in the binary system, you always start with 0. Next is a 1. But what do you do after that? Think back to powers of 2. Every digit you see can be assigned a power of 2, and these can be switched "on," when they have a 1, or "off," when they have a 0. Then you add together all the columns that have 1s in them. So for 10 (= 2 in our normal way of counting), you divide 10 into two columns. The column on the right is 2^0 and the column on the left is 2^1. Only the left column is turned "on," because it is a 1. That is the only column you count. You know that 2^1 is 2, and that is your answer.

For 3, both columns are now turned on. From right to left, you have $2^0 + 2^1 = 3$. For 4, you now have a 2^3 column. Only that column is turned on, and $2^3 = 4$.

2. How would you explain the number 8? And 9?

There are 8 bits in a byte. With 8 bits, values in a byte can range from 00000000 to 11111111. (There are 8 options for a 1 or 0.)

3. What value would the byte 11001000 be?

6
WRITING IN BINARY

AJ continues to explain more about binary, bits, and bytes, and what it all actually means. He asks Teresa to open up Word Pad, the most basic text program on their computer. He asks her to type out her name, which she does.

"What do you see?" he asks her. Teresa says she just sees the letters that make up her name. But AJ says that to the computer, the letters look like binary code. The computer can only read 1s and 0s, not letters. The computer reads each character on the screen as 1 byte (8 bits). Then he shows her how to write in binary, without using any letters! Learn how on the next pages.

Each character (letter or symbol, like a period or dash) on the screen is 1 byte of information to a computer.

People have come up with a system where each character is assigned a particular byte code. For example:

$$A = 010000001$$
$$B = 010000010$$
$$C = 010000011$$

1. What is A, B, and C if you convert it into normal (decimal) numbers?

You need to know which numbers—in either binary or decimal—match up with which characters to be able to write in binary.

When Teresa writes out her name, the bytes of information in binary code she is using are:

$$T = 01010100$$
$$E = 01100101$$
$$R = 01110010$$
$$E = 01100101$$
$$S = 01110011$$
$$A = 01100001$$

2. What is each letter in decimal numbers?

3. If Teresa's last name starts with the byte represented by 72, which of the following letters is that?

$$M = 01001101$$
$$D = 01000100$$
$$H = 01001000$$

7
CONVERTING TO HEXADECIMAL

AJ tells Teresa that there's another kind of number that computers understand other than binary: hexadecimal. Just like binary numbers are base 2 and the normal numbers we use are base 10, hexadecimal numbers are base 16. This means that there are more digits than we have numerals for, since our writing system only has ten numerals! The computer starts using letters after 9, so it has enough symbols. Here's how you write the numbers 1 to 16 in hexadecimal:

1 = 1	9 = 9
2 = 2	A = 10
3 = 3	B = 11
4 = 4	C = 12
5 = 5	D = 13
6 = 6	E = 14
7 = 7	F = 15
8 = 8	10 = 16

You can convert between binary and hexadecimal pretty easily. Since 16 is the same as 2^4, every four digits of binary works out to one digit of hexadecimal.

Binary	Decimal	Hexadecimal
0001	1	1
0101	5	5
1010	10	A
1011	11	B
1100	12	C
1101	13	D
1111	15	F

1. What's the binary number 1001 in hexadecimal?

2. What's the hexadecimal number 1A in base 10?

3. What's the hexadecimal number C1 in binary?

8
COMPUTER LOGIC

Soon after she starts at her new school, Teresa has to do a research. She has to research her town's history. She doesn't really know much about her new town, so she has to do a lot of research.

She starts by using Google. First, she searches for "Brookeville," the name of her town. She gets a lot of results, but most of them don't have anything to do with her town. She wonders how to search so she only gets the results she wants. Her project would be a lot easier if she could narrow down her search results.

Luckily, there is an easy way to do that. She can use a Boolean search. Boolean logic involves the terms "and," "or," and "not." Boolean searches are part of a system of logic that computers use all the time. You can use it for Google searches, but computers use it to do everyday functions too.

First, Teresa could just add another term to her search. Brookeville is in New York State, so she could search for "Brookeville New York." She doesn't have to put the "and" in there, because Google assumes you mean "and." This search will produce results that contain both the words Brookeville and New York.

Teresa notices a lot of her results are for Brookevilles in other states, especially Texas. She could search for "Brookeville –Texas." The minus sign before Texas means "not" in Google search terms. Now, she leaves out results with the word Texas.

The town also used to be called Brooketon a long time ago. Teresa can search for both Brookeville and Brooketon at once by searching for "Brookeville OR Brooketon." The "or" returns results that contain either or the other.

Computers use this logic too, just not in word form. They use 1s and 0s, of course. You can use tables to show the logic. Here is a table for an AND command, and the explanation. In this table, A is the first input, B is the second input, and Q is the output. The only way for Q to be 1 is for both A and B to be 1.

A B Q
0 0 0 *If A is 0 AND B is 0, Q is 0.*
0 1 0 *If A is 0 AND B is 1, Q is 0.*
1 0 0 *If A is 1 AND B is 0, Q is 0.*
1 1 1

1. What would 1 1 1 mean in an AND table?

   The OR table looks like this. If either A or B is 1, the output will be 1. Fill in the rest of the explanations.

2. **A B Q**
   0 0 0 If A is 0 and B is 0, Q is 0.
   0 1 1
   1 0 1
   1 1 1

   Here is the NOT table. There is only one input, and the output is always the opposite.

   A Q
   0 1
   1 0

3. What would Teresa's "Brooketon –Texas" search look like in computer terms? You can think of it as searching for "Brooketon AND NOT Texas," which eliminates results from a Brooketon AND Texas search.

9
BASIC PROGRAMMING

Teresa is starting to make some good friends at her new school. One of her new friends, Mel, happens to be really good at computers.

One day, when Mel is over at Teresa's house, Teresa mentions her calculator ran out of batteries and she hasn't had time to get new ones yet. Mel tells her she shouldn't worry about her calculator because she can just turn her computer into a calculator for math.

Teresa will need to learn a little programming first, Mel explains. Programming is how you tell computers commands, kind of like another language you need to know to work with computers. The computer will translate the programming commands, called programming code, into binary numbers, so the computer recognizes what you're telling it to do. Mel has already studied programming a little bit, so she shows Teresa what to do.

There are hundreds of different programming languages. It doesn't really matter which one you use, as long as you follow the rules for that language. All of the examples in this section are a made-up language that could exist. The computer languages you know or learn will look a little different, but they'll do the same things.

Mel tells Teresa that all computer programs are divided into coding lines. Each line has one command. Programs have to start by telling the computer a program is running and that it is ending, like this:

1 Program
2 End Program

What you put between the two commands are the instructions for the computer to become a calculator, or run whatever program you want.

Teresa's math homework involves a lot of cubed numbers, which are numbers times themselves three times. Think back to binary numbers and powers of 2. Two cubed is 2^3, or 2 x 2 x 2. Teresa wants her computer program to calculate numbers cubed.

Here are the steps. Remember, the first is "Program" and the last is "End Program":

First, they have to tell the computer to make space to store the number they are cubing and the number cubed, before they even writes the code for cubing. This is called declaring a **variable**. Our variable will be called "xCubed." You can make a new variable by deciding what kind of information will be stored in it (text or a number) and naming the variable. For example, "Number (xCubed)" will make a new number variable named xCubed.

Next, Mel tells Teresa she will have to tell the computer to cube the number 2 by multiplying it three times, and put the resulting value into "xCubed."

Finally, Teresa has to tell the computer to give the answer to the cube equation in the seventh line. She can have it print out the answer in words.

1. Rearrange these lines of computer code in the order you think they should go, to tell the computer how to calculate square roots. The words not in parentheses are the commands, the symbols in parentheses **modify** the commands.

   Print "This program will find the result of the equation 2^3."
   End Program
   Program
   Number (xCubed)
   Print "Your number cubed is ", (xCubed)
   (xCubed= 2 * 2 * 2)

10
WEBSITE DESIGN: PIXELS

Now Teresa wants to create her own website to communicate with her friends in her old town. She's so busy all the time that she doesn't always have time to call or e-mail them all individually. A website with updates about herself would be a good way to stay in touch with all her friends at once.

Teresa is using a website-building program that makes it a little easier. She still has to make decisions about what she wants her site to look like. For example, she needs to pick the right dimensions. She doesn't want her site to be too big for the page, or too small.

Websites are measured in pixels, just like other things are measured in inches, centimeters, or miles. One pixel is a tiny dot that makes up an image on a computer screen. One image is made up of thousands or millions of pixels. The pixels are so small that you can't see them individually—they all blend together into a smooth picture. A good website will have the right dimensions, so it looks nice.

When you pick the number of pixels you want a website to be, you choose between options that look like this:

640 x 480
1024 x 768
800 x 600

In other words, a website that is 640 x 480 is 640 pixels across the width of the screen, and 480 pixels along the height. This number is called the resolution.

You calculate the number of pixels on that website the same way you calculate area, by multiplying the length and the width.

1. How many pixels are in a 640 x 480 website?

2. Which has more pixels, a website that is 1024 x 768 or 1280 x 800? How many more?

A good website will have resolutions that match the most people's computer screens. If your computer's resolution is 800 x 600, but you're looking at a website that is 1024 x 768, the website is bigger. You won't be able to see it all on one screen. You'll have to scroll to the right to see the whole website.

Teresa takes a poll of her friends. She asks them what resolution their computer screens are, so she can pick the right resolution for her website. These are the results:

800 x 600 = 2 people
1024 x 768 = 6 people
1280 x 800 = 1 person

3. Which computer screen resolution should Teresa try to match? Why?

11
WEBSITE DESIGN: COLORS

Next, Teresa has to pick some colors for her website. As she's picking colors on the website design program, she notices that each color has a funny number that identifies it. The number actually contains a bunch of numerals, but also some letters. She notices a purplish color, for example, is C030FF. What does it mean?

Teresa is looking at a way of counting called hexadecimal. Like binary, hexadecimal is just a different way of thinking about counting. We normally use a system called decimal, based on the number 10. Binary is based on the number 2. Hexadecimal is based on 16. It has the ten numerals 0 through 9. And instead of making up new symbols for the rest of the numbers, hexadecimal uses the six letters A through F.

To get the hexadecimal code for a color, you're really combining 3 different hexadecimal numbers. The C0 in the purple is how much red is in the color. The 30 is how much green there is. And FF is how much blue there is.

You will need to better understand how to count in hexadecimal first.

The first 16 numbers in hexadecimal are 0, 1, 2, 3, 4, 5, 6, 7, 8, 9, A, B, C, D, E, F.

After that, is:

$$10 \ (= 16)$$
$$11 \ (= 17)$$
$$12 \ (= 18)$$

What is going on? Remember back to binary, when you learned that each column in the number equals 2 to a power. The same is true of hexadecimal, except that you are working with powers of 16, not powers of 2.

10 really means $1 \times 16^1 + 0 \times 16^0$, which equals 16.

1. What does 14 equal, using powers of 16?

   You will need to remember which values A through F equal.

   The number 4C, is really $4 \times 16^1 + 12 \times 16^0$. C is 12 in hexadecimal. So 4C equals 64 + 12, or 76.

For colors, computers always mix together red, green, and blue, in that order. Green already contains yellow, which is how the computer can get yellow. Each color has a two-digit hexadecimal code. That's why each color actually has 6 digits, because it is combining 3 colors. The first two numbers tell you how much red is in the color, the second set of 2 numbers tell you how much green/yellow there is, and the third set of 2 numbers tells you how much blue there is.

2. What color would you expect E41D14 to be?

The lower the number, the darker (closer to black it is). The higher the number, the closer to white it is: 000000 is black, while FFFFFF is white.

3. Would the blue value E9 be closer to black or white? Why?

That purple color Teresa chose was C030FF. Now you have to deal with powers of 16, 0 through 5, because there are 5 columns of numbers.

4. What is the purple color's value in the decimal system?

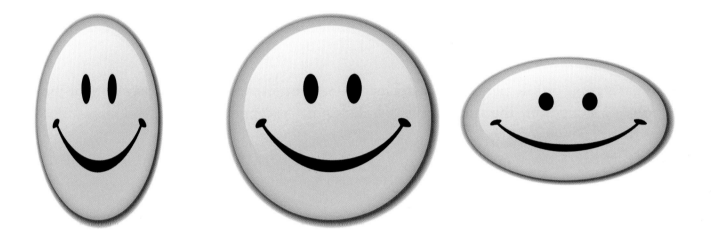

12
WEBSITE DESIGN: PROPORTION

Teresa's website is halfway done, but she still has to add images and text boxes to it. She has a whole list of things she wants to include, but she has to make sure it all fits on each web-page. To fit everything, she has to play around with the size of each image or text box.

Teresa quickly discovers that she is dealing with **proportions**. When she changes an image size, for example, she could choose to change it proportionally. As she makes the image wider, she also makes it longer, which keeps the image looking normal, just bigger. She could also change it disproportionally, by making it too wide or too long. That makes it look squished. Understanding proportions makes website design easier, and makes websites look a lot nicer.

Two things that are proportional have the same relationship. A picture that is 3 inches by 6 inches has a specific relationship between its length (3 inches) and height (6 inches). You can give that relationship as a fraction:

$$\frac{\text{width}}{\text{length}}$$

$$\frac{3 \text{ inches}}{6 \text{ inches}}$$

Teresa wants the pictures she's putting on the website to be larger than 3 inches by 6 inches. However, she wants it to look the same and have the same proportions, rather than get squished.

In fact, she wants the picture to be 5 inches in width. To find the new length, you have to find the fraction that has the same relationship between width and length as the original picture. You already know that relationship is ³⁄₆.

Set the two picture size proportions equal to each other, leaving out the missing information. Add an X for the measurement you don't know.

$$\frac{3}{6} = \frac{5}{x}$$

Now cross-multiply:

1. 3 x X = 5 x 6
    X =

2. If Teresa wanted to make the height of the text box an inch smaller, what would the new, proportional width and height be?

3. Which of these screen resolutions is proportional to 1024 x 768? (There may be more than one answer.)

    a. 960 x 720
    b. 976 x 580
    c. 1080 x 925
    d. 1140 x 855

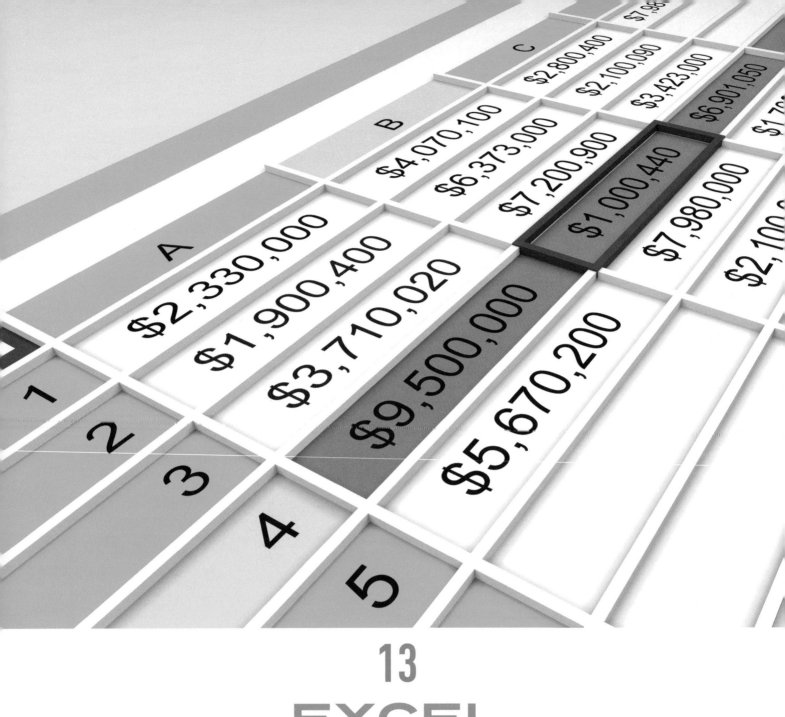

13
EXCEL

Teresa's computer has Excel on it, a program she uses from time to time for school projects. She could even use Excel for that history project she was working on before, about the history of her new town.

The second part of her project asks how many people have lived in the town over the years. Teresa could just do the research and write down all the numbers she finds for each year, but she wants to take it a step further. She decides to type all her information into Excel and make it into a graph representing the population of her town. See what the chart and graph look like on the next page.

This is what Teresa types into an Excel chart, which will be made into a graph.

Year	Population
1750	45
1775	231
1800	879
1825	1,670
1850	4,006
1875	7,096
1900	10,213
1925	10,607
1950	10,890
1975	9,992
2000	8,863
2025	?

1. What should the x-axis on Teresa's graph be labeled? What about the y-axis?

Here is what the graph looks like. Add in the axis labels.

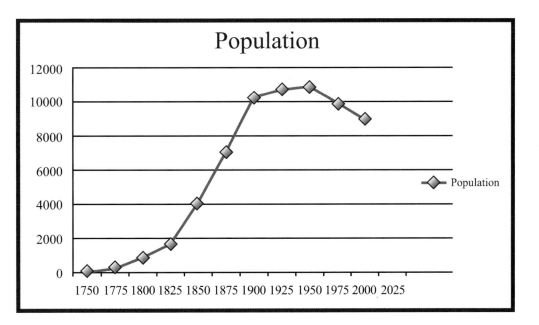

You can **estimate** what the 2025 population will be with this graph. Just draw or imagine a line extending out with the same **slope** as what has come right before. The point at which your line crosses the year is your estimate.

2. What do you estimate the population will be in 2025?

14
MORE EXCEL

Excel is a great program for doing math on a computer, as Teresa is discovering. Besides making graphs, Teresa can use it to make calculations with the **data** she has entered into a chart.

Teresa wants to find the average number of people who have lived in her town over the years. Finding the average is easy on Excel, and Teresa won't even have to pick up a calculator.

Here is what Teresa's Excel chart looks like, with the columns and rows labeled:

	A	B	C
1	Year	Year	Population
2	1750	45	
3	1775	231	
4	1800	879	
5	1825	1,670	
6	1850	4,006	
7	1875	7,096	
8	1900	10,213	
9	1925	10,607	
10	1950	10,890	
11	1975	9,992	
12	2000	8,863	
13	2025	?	

To do calculations in Excel, you have to know how to write functions. Functions are just things you do to data to get an answer. In math, the function for average is adding up all the numbers you're averaging and dividing by how many numbers you added. Excel already knows how to average numbers, so all you have to do is tell Excel you want an average.

Teresa types in =AVERAGE(B2:B12) in an empty cell in column C. The word AVERAGE tells Excel she wants to find the average. She also has to tell it what numbers she wants to average. Those numbers are in cells B2 to B12.

1. What is the average population between 1750 and 2000? You can use Excel or a calculator (or do it in your head).

2. What would you type if you wanted to only find the average of the years 1900 to 2000?

Teresa could also find the difference between different populations. If she wanted to see how much the population had grown from 1750 to 2000, she would type this into an empty cell:

=B12 – B2

3. What would she type if she wanted to know the difference between the years 1950 and 1850?

15
PUTTING IT ALL TOGETHER

Moving to a new town was a new start for Teresa, as far as computers are concerned. She has learned a lot about Internet speed, binary numbers, programming, and more. See if you can remember some of what she has learned.

1. Your Internet speed is 30mbs/4 mbs.

   How long would it take a file that is 11 megabytes to download?

   How long would it take the file to upload?

2. How many bits are in a terabyte?

3. You have used up 35% of your e-mail program's storage of 20.5 megabytes. How many megabytes of storage do you have left?

4. What is the binary number 1011010011?

5. In an AND computer operation, what will Q be if A is 1 and B is 0?

   What will Q be with the same inputs, but an OR operation?

6. How many pixels are on a website that is 890 x 720?

   Will someone with a 640 x 480-sized screen be able to see the website well? Why or why not?

7. What is the hexadecimal number F2193A in decimal form?

What color is that closest to—red, green/yellow, or blue? Why?

8. You are resizing a text box that was originally 2.4 inches wide and 7.5 inches long. You want it to stay proportional, but be 3.4 inches wide.

How long will the text box be?

FIND OUT MORE IN BOOKS

Coussement, Frank and Peter De Schepper. *Baffling Binary Puzzles.* Watertown, Mass.: Charlesbridge Publishing, 2009.

DK Publishing. *Computer.* New York: DK Publishing, 2011.

Sande, Warren and Carter Sande. *Hello World! Computer Programming for Kids and Other Beginners.* Greenwich, Conn.: Manning Publications, 2013.

Selfridge, Benjamin and Peter Selfridge. *A Kid's Guide to Creating Web Pages for Home and School.* Chicago, Ill.: Zephyr Press, 2004.

FIND OUT MORE
ON THE INTERNET

Binary/Decimal/Hexadecimal Converter
www.mathsisfun.com/binary-decimal-hexadecimal-converter.html

Coecademy: Basic Computer Programming
www.codecademy.com/#!/exercises/0

Computer Storage Converter
www.convert-me.com/en/convert/computer

Excel Tutorial
sunburst.usd.edu/~bwjames/tut/excel

Hexadecimal Colors
www.mathsisfun.com/hexadecimal-decimal-colors.html

Scratch: Basic Computer Programming
scratch.mit.edu

Glossary

Convert: to change from one thing to another.

Data: information, especially in number form.

Dimensions: the measurements of length, width (and possibly depth) that describe an object.

Estimate: make an educated guess.

Expressed: represented by.

Graphic design: using text and information to communicate information.

Input: information that is entered.

Logic: a system of reasoning.

Modify: describe.

Notation: a system of symbols used to represent numbers or other values.

Output: information that is produced or supplied.

Proportions: parts thought about in comparison to the whole, ratios.

Range: the area between upper and lower limits.

Slope: the inclination of a line.

Transfer: to move from one place to another.

Variable: a symbol or word used in the place of a number whose value you don't know or might change.

ANSWERS

1.

1. 512/ 8 = 64 kilobytes per second, 980 kilobytes/64 kilobytes per second = 15.31 seconds
2. Both are more than a second; you would likely notice the difference.

2.

1. 175.54 seconds (560 ÷ 8 = 70 kilobytes per second, 12 x 1024 = 12288 kilobytes, 12288 ÷ 70 = 175.54 seconds)
   48 seconds (2 ÷ 8 = .25 megabytes per second, 12 ÷.25 = 48 seconds)
   96 seconds (1 ÷ 8 = .125 megabytes per second, 12 ÷.125 = 96 seconds)
   768 seconds (128 ÷ 8 = 16 kilobytes per second, 12 x 1024 = 12288 kilobytes, 12288 ÷ 16 = 768 seconds)
   19.2 seconds (5 ÷ 8 = .625 megabytes per second, 12 ÷.625 = 19.2 seconds)
2. Standard: 10.67 ÷ 160 seconds
   Extra: 5.33 ÷ 32 seconds
   Ultra: 3.2 ÷ 32 seconds
3. They should choose the extra package; they will probably not notice the difference too much in download speeds.

3.

1. 1 gigabyte x 1024 megabytes x 1024 kilobytes = 1,048,576 kilobytes
2. 3 exabytes x 1024 petabytes x 1024 terabytes = 3,145,728
3. 89 x 8 = 712 bits

4.

1. .80 x 10.1 = 8.08 gigabytes used; 10.1 − 8.08 = 2.03 gigabytes left
2. 100 x X = 80 x 10.1, X = 8.08 gigabytes left; yes, same answer
3. 8.08 x 1024 = 8273.92 kilobytes
4. 1924 ÷ 1024 = 1.88 gigabytes, 8.08 − 1.88 = 6.2 gigabytes; 6.2/10.1 = X/100, X = 61.39%

5.

1. 2 x 2 x 2 x 2 x 2 x 2 x 2 = 128
2. $2^4 + 0 + 0 + 0 = 8$, $2^4 + 0 + 0 + 2^0 = 9$
3. $2^7 + 2^6 + 0 + 0 + 2^3 + 0 + 0 + 0 = 128 + 64 + 8 = 200$
4. 1024 x 8 = 8192 options.

6.

1. 65, 66, 67
2. 84, 101, 114, 101, 115, 97
3. H = 01001000

7.

1. 9
2. 26
3. 11000001

8.

1. If A is 1 AND B is 1, Q is 1.
2. A B Q
   0 0 0 If A is 0 and B is 0, Q is 0.
   0 1 1 If A is 0 and B is 1, Q is 1.
   1 0 1 If A is 1 and B is 0, Q is 1
   1 1 1 If A is 1 and B is 1, Q is 1
3. A = 1, B = 0

9.

Program
Number (xCubed)
Print "This program will find the result of the equation 2^3."
(xCubed= 2 * 2 * 2)
Print "Your number cubed is ", (xCubed)
End Program

10.

1. 307,200 pixels
2. 1280 x 800; 237,568 more
3. 1024 x 768, because most of her friends have that resolution.

11.

1. $1 \times 16^1 + 4 \times 16^0 = 20$
2. Red
3. Closer to white, because it is a high number.
4. $12 \times 165 + 0 \times 164 + 3 \times 163 + 0 \times 162 + 15 \times 161 + 15 \times 160 = 12,595,456$

12.

1. 10 inches
2. $3/6 = 2/X$, X = 4 inches
3. a, d

13.

1. The x-axis is Year and the y-axis is Population
2. Around 8,000.

14.

1. 5,862.91
2. =AVERAGE(B8:B12)
3. =B10-B6

15.

1. $30/8 = 3.75$ megabytes per second; 11 megabytes/3.75 megabytes per second = 2.93 seconds
   $4/8 = .5$ megabytes per second; 11 megabytes/$.5$ megabytes per second = 22 seconds
2. $1 \times 1024 \times 1024 \times 1024 \times 1024 \times 8 = 8,796,093,022,208$
3. $.35 \times 20.5 = 7.175$, $20.5 - 7.175 = 13.325$ megabytes
4. 723

5. 0; 1
6. 640,800; No, because their screen is smaller than the website.
7. 15866170; Red, because the highest values are in the two red columns of the number.
8. $2.4/7.5 = 3.4/X$, X = 10.625 inches

Index

About the Author

James Fischer received his master's in education from the State University of New York, and went on to teach life skills to middle school students with learning disabilities. He has also written books for the Mason Crest series, Junior Library of Money.

Picture Credits